HOW THE QUEEN CAN MAKE YOU HAPPY

HOW THE QUEEN CAN MAKE YOU HAPPY

First published 2012 by Elliott and Thompson Limited
27 John Street, London WC1N 2BX
www.eandtbooks.com

ISBN: 978-1-908739-14-8

Text © Mary Killen 2012

Quotations on pages 83 and 107 © Kahlil Gibran, *The Prophet*
(William Heinnemann, 1926)

9 8 7 6 5 4 3 2 1

A CIP catalogue record for this book is available from
the British Library.

Printed and bound in the UK by CPI Group (UK) Ltd,
Croydon CR0 4YY

Typeset by PDQ Media

Image credits
Hong Kong and Australia stamps © Lefteris Papaulakis /
Shutterstock.com
South Africa stamp © Snap2Art / Shutterstock.com
UK stamp (50p) © MarkauMark / Shutterstock.com
UK stamp (2½D) © Neftali / Shutterstock.com

Every effort has been made to trace copyright holders for
extracts used within this book. Where this has not been
possible, the publisher will be happy to credit them in future
editions.

For Blossom Barrow, who never met the
Queen but had her own kingdom

Contents

Introduction

'Throughout the world and with all
due respect to every other female
monarch, whenever we speak about
the Queen, we all know which one
we are referring to.'

Ronald Reagan, 1991

She has been seen in person by more of her
subjects and has spoken to more of her subjects
than any previous monarch. Yet whether these
conversations are long or short, she remains
an enigma to all those outside her inner circle.

But what are the secrets that make her tick?
Why, at the age of 86, is she still fit enough to
ride for four days a week and walk her dogs for

half an hour each day after lunch in the Palace gardens? How is it that she is still fit enough to fulfil an average of 370 public engagements a year, in addition to receiving 50,000 guests a year in Buckingham Palace as well as foreign leaders for weeklong state visits while missing just a handful of engagements throughout her whole reign?

How is it that Her Majesty's brain still works well enough for her to process with speed and clarity upwards of 10,000 words of complex state papers per day? And where does she find the strength to keep calm and carry on?

To all these and other queries, you will find answers within. As you read, the onion skins will be pared away to reveal the truth, which was always obvious – if you only had eyes to see – of how the Queen can make you happy.

Compartmentalizing

'Man was made for joy and woe', observed William Blake, adding words to the effect that, once we accept that's the nature of being alive and stop taking the setbacks personally, 'then through life we safely go'. Betty Parsons, the late childbirth expert and fountain of wisdom, agreed when she said, 'Life is a jigsaw', and that, 'At the end of it, you look back and see that you cannot separate the dark pieces from the light – they go together.'

Mrs Parsons is known to have been integral to royal pregnancies, including the Queen's with Prince Edward. She never divulged a detail, but the royal patronage assumes an accordance with the 20,000 other women who attended Betty

Parsons' London clinic between 1963 and 1986, and who believed that she was far more than a 'birth guru'. In fact her words had a resonance of truth to the extent that most of Betty's 'girls' report that, even now, they continue to hear her voice telling them what to do.

At Betty's ninetieth birthday party at Brooks's Club, St James's, in 2005, women she had not seen for decades swarmed in to pay tribute and lined up to tell her 'what you taught me for childbirth was so helpful, but what you taught me for life was invaluable.' One of the nuggets of wisdom our Queen would have learnt from Mrs Parsons is, 'Plan for tomorrow, but *live* in today'. In other words, there is no use 'catastrophizing' about what disasters may lie in store. Disasters are part of life – but so are enjoyments. Enjoy.

The Queen could be in mourning every day of her life. For over 86 years she has had social access to top-of-the-range human specimens from all points of the globe, and these crème de la crème must die off at the rate of about five a day. Imagine having to cope with serially losing people of the standard of Sir Winston Churchill and Ted Hughes, OM, the Poet Laureate. But as Churchill himself pronounced, 'If you are going through hell, keep going.' On the afternoon of the death of her sister, Princess Margaret, the Queen was visiting Great Ormond Street Hospital for Children to celebrate its 150th anniversary. She was clad in black but smiling.

How does she do it? She compartmentalizes. Her philosophy seems to be, there may be trouble ahead and behind but, at this precise moment, I am enjoying doing something useful and cheering people up so I will concentrate on that.

Clearly, she plans for tomorrow but lives in today.

Moving constantly between houses and palaces helps to inculcate compartmentalizing, not only of the different aspects of life but also of the people in it. If a guest is particularly tiresome, they won't be there for long – and neither will you. If they are fabulous, like Sir David Attenborough, anyone would make the most of every second. Of course we can't all move constantly between palaces but we can get away from *ourselves* by going to stay with friends. What blessed relief to get away from the physical objects that remind us of our problems and undone chores. By going away, we too can learn to compartmentalize. Distance lends enchantment and perspective and, no matter how humble your hovel, you can play your part in the Big Society by inviting people to stay with you. Let them get away from *themselves*.

Your own premises need not be four star. It is widely observed that, unless there is a food-poisoning risk, few people mind eating or sleeping in chaotic houses owned by their friends. On the contrary, they almost prefer a friend's house to offer inferior standards of comfort to their own. They can then gain a warm glow of superiority as they count the blessings of their own more streamlined homes.

Concentration

Concentration is a lot easier for a member of the *Vieillesse dorée* – the Grade One generation from which the Queen hails; they were born in the days when all food was organic and before flashing lights and swiftly changing images on screens had corrupted the brain's ability to make dopamine as a reward for concentration.

The brain is a muscle and it responds to use. The Queen has always read all her briefing papers and, at 86, is unfailingly up to speed. In order to keep your own brain fit for purpose, like the Queen you also need to shut out distractions. Concentration – almost a lost art – is not just useful for processing paperwork and making decisions, it is also a remarkably useful social skill. How else could the Queen deal with, say, an investiture of more than 100 people in less than 90 minutes and leave none of them feeling short-changed? Her secret is to properly engage so that, even though she may move on from person to person about every 60 seconds, or even less, each gong-winner is left with the sense of having commanded their monarch's full attention.

Never was such a skill more highly valued than today. No one likes being on the receiving – or should it be the withholding – end of the sort of behaviour that requires us to queue for someone's attention as they first process the demands of their mobile and their apps. (Ed Balls was apparently even seen checking his emails in company when a guest at Windsor Castle.)

Anyone can learn the skill of concentration; it requires only practice, and the rewards are well worth the effort. We have all come across someone enjoying a mysterious social or romantic success while appearing, on the surface, to have nothing going for them whatsoever. 'Yes,' breathe the members of their fan club, 'but they are so incredibly charismatic. When you talk to them, it's as though you are the only person in the room.'

It was Dale Carnegie, author of *How to Win Friends and Influence People*, who first identified the key secret of social success – listening, and not being distracted while you do so. He described a famously popular man who rarely said a word in conversation, except to prompt his interlocutor. Invariably, as the man walked away, the latter would turn to someone else and say, 'That was the most fascinating person I ever met in my life!'

Don't misunderstand, I am not saying that the Queen is insincere. On the contrary, her magic is entirely linked to the fact that she genuinely *is* interested. It is your duty to become so too.

Continuity

'It is a question of maturing into something that one's got used to doing, and accepting the fact that it's your fate, because I think that continuity is very important.'
The Queen in a BBC documentary, 1992

The vast galaxy in which we live is spinning at the incredible speed of 490,000mph. Even at this breakneck speed our galaxy still needs 200 million years to make just one rotation. And while the planets make their predictable round of the heavens, down below the Queen can be relied upon to be in a certain place, at a certain time of year, every year. So ...

Autumn: Buckingham Palace
Christmas: Windsor Castle
January/February: Sandringham
Easter: Windsor Castle
Early summer: Holyroodhouse
Summer: Balmoral Castle

Furthermore, for 15 minutes of the Queen's breakfast every morning a Pipe Major from the Argyll and Sutherland Highlanders marches outside the Queen's dining room playing the bagpipes (a tradition started by Queen Victoria in 1843). Changing of the Guard always takes place at exactly 11.30am. And at Trooping the Colour, the Queen's birthday parade, the clock in Horse Guards Parade is adjusted to ensure that it strikes 11 exactly as the Queen enters the parade ground.

Like her or not, she serves as a focus for national unity, not to mention continuity. It is also useful for us to have a Head of State whose authority remains unaffected by government failure. A monarch who reigns without ruling enables at least one institution to inspire popular trust. So, while times and people move on, the Queen is always there as a totem of reassurance and the eternal verities. She reassures us with her presence while at the same time adapting and moving in tandem with change.

While simultaneously endorsing many quaint traditions – for example, barristers dress as they do because they are still in mourning for Queen Mary who died in 1694, and Etonians because they are in mourning for George III – she opens up Buckingham Palace for public scrutiny, allows the gardens to be used for rock concerts and permits her son and heir to become yet another grocer in this nation of shopkeepers.

So, embrace continuity as part of your lifestyle but don't take things too far, as did Scottish landowner John Ouchterlony of The Guynd, near Arbroath where, for more than 400 years, each successive male laird has sat on the same furniture looking out through the same windows of the Georgian mansion at the same unchanging view. Ouchterlony was so resistant to change of any kind – even though money and light would have cascaded into the mansion if he had allowed Belinda Rathbone, his dynamic American wife, to move with the times – that he drove her back to America. (The full tale is recounted in her instructive 2005 memoir, *Living with the Laird*.) Ouchterlony's mistake was to conflate continuity with former grandeur.

However, benign continuity is a different matter. When planning holidays, we could take our lead from the Queen, as do various notables. The late Sir John Betjeman went to Trebetherick in Cornwall every year of his life and said he always felt safe once he had crossed the Tamar. There is a lot to be said for knowing exactly what the score is – what the weather will be like, who else is likely to be around, which roads are dangerous and where you are likely to be beaten up or sucked out to sea. Once you have 'learned the ropes' of people and places, it frees you to get on with other activities.

Remember being at school and checking the term dates? Admit it, far from being oppressive or restricting, it was liberating to know the boundaries. Just think of all the time freed up in not having to look at catalogues or websites to choose a new holiday destination, all the while wondering what the hidden defects might be. Moreover, doing the same things each year helps you to monitor your progress and compete against yourself. Last year I was able to climb Snowdonia; if I can't do it again this year, I will have to go to the gym when I get back. No one place (or person) is necessarily better than any other, but repeated exposure to each helps you to get the best out of both. Also, in today's hectic world, one of the ways to filter or control the barrage of stuff coming at us is to have non-negotiable timetables. 'We always go to Consett for the first two weeks of August,' you can tell those trying to invade your space.

And as for continuity of marital partner, don't divorce. There won't be anyone better. Every domestic partner is annoying these days. Better stick with the devil you know – the children far prefer it and you can go slowly downhill together with your shared memories of the days when you were young and fit for purpose. Just think how wonderful it is to have a live-in prompt to remind you of people's names from 50 years ago. Of course the Queen is so busy that she need not see too much of her own husband if she does not want to, though apparently they get on extremely well. Incidentally, of the irritable-seeming Duke who apparently suffers no fools gladly, the late Commander Michael Parker, his private secretary and close friend for 60 years, has revealed, 'no one has a kinder heart nor takes more trouble to conceal it'.

But for those of us who are trapped in small houses with irritating husbands, and who just want to ride out a decade or two until nature takes its course, the thing to do is to simply start going to bed four or five hours before or after he does, and ditto with getting up. Then you only need to see him for seven hours a day – surely that's manageable?

Digestion

Sitting up straight at a table with a ramrod posture, as if with a book on your head, is unfashionable these days. But there was a health agenda driving the tradition that saw generations of children strapped into straitjackets until they had learned to sit up properly. The junior Queen Victoria was even made to wear a sprig of holly on her neck while eating, to ensure that she sat up properly and looked straight ahead.

Correct deportment was considered the cornerstone of good health for a reason, and not just because it eliminates back injuries, which afflict one-third of Britons at some time. Sitting and standing up straight is the best way to ensure your food can be digested. The intestines are lengthy and they have been carefully designed by nature to include villi, miniscule projections that propel the food through to its natural exit point.

If the intestines are compromised or cramped through people sitting hunched, in a bunched posture or lolling on low sofas choking down TV dinners like dogs, it doesn't happen. The food gets stuck. In addition, it gets stuck because bread made with the Chorleywood method (i.e. most bread these days), which dispenses with proper fermentation, contains more gluten than in the days when bread was the staff of life. Gluten is a chewing gum-style substance which coats the villi and stops them sweeping through the food. Thus there is a traffic jam inside. The Queen does not eat improperly fermented bread and her gut is not cluttered with undigested debris.

Incidentally, the gut (or intestinal system) is now acknowledged to be far more powerful than we realized. Indeed, it has its own 'brain' and can operate independently of the brain 'up top'. (If you want to know more, then check out London nutritionist Gudrun Jonsson and American Dr Michael D. Gershon, author of *The Second Brain*, who are pioneers of gut therapy.)

Antibiotics can also disrupt inner workings, leading to a 'toxic gut'. The Queen does not take antibiotics and believes in homeopathy, using arsenic to prevent sneezing, onions to deal with a runny nose and deadly nightshade to deal with a sore throat. (The royals were introduced to homeopathy in the 1920s by Sir John Weir, who was succeeded by Dr Margery Blackie, also a royal physician.)

Finally, don't forget that eating with your mouth shut is in the top ten of standard British good manners. Besides the aesthetics, it's necessary to avoid gulping in air while you eat because it causes gas blockages in the digestion process. It's not funny or attractive – you will never hear the Queen burping, even after she had to swallow Fiji's national soap-like Yaqona drink in one draught, as etiquette demanded, while on a state visit there in 1977.

Dignity

In 1956 the Queen Mother's racehorse Devon Loch collapsed and died within inches of the winning post in the Grand National. The racing fanatic's spontaneous response was to turn to the Duke of Devonshire and say, 'I must go down and comfort those poor people,' and she went immediately to the jockey, Dick Francis, the trainer and the stable lads. 'It was the most perfect display of dignity that I have ever witnessed,' remarked the Duke.

Even when physical incapacity strikes, the royals can show how to retain dignity. The 15-year-old Prince Philip, visiting Athens for the first time since his infancy for the state reinternment of his relations, who had died in exile from Greece, was suddenly overcome with nausea and vomited into his new top hat. And remember how the Queen kept her cool when Michael Fagan, an unemployed father of four, broke into her bedchamber in July 1982 while the footman on guard was out walking the dogs in the Palace gardens? According to reports at the time, Fagan sat on her bed talking to her for about ten minutes before help arrived.

It is by no means the only unstately experience she has had. The first time the Queen met baronet and garden designer Roddy Llewellyn was on a Saturday evening at Royal Lodge. The Queen was talking to a nanny in the nursery when Mr Llewellyn burst in, wearing only a shirt and underpants and hoping to have buttons sewn on. 'Please forgive me ma'am. I look awful,' he said. 'Don't worry, I don't look too good myself,' replied the Queen. The next day they were formally introduced after both had attended Chapel at Windsor.

Can those of us whose spontaneous response to such incidents would be a show of disgrace under pressure, screaming like fishwives or laughing hysterically, learn to be dignified? Not without having a spiritual element to our lives and a sense of perspective.

You can control some aspects of your image, though. Think in the long, rather than short, term. As a teenager, for example, you could mark yourself out from the crowd by being the only one of your generation not to upload embarrassing photos of yourself on to social networking sites. Why not ban friends from taking photographs at social gatherings in your house? Try it once and see how relaxed everyone becomes. And crucially avoid, as the Queen does, being photographed while eating or drinking. She is constantly being urged to try various biscuits and cakes that people offer her when she is 'touring' food emporiums – 'They look very nice,' she replies, but does not take one.

Of course women can't all have dressers – as the royals call ladies' maids – but royal clothing tips include sewing wind-resistant weights into the hems of skirts and kilts so that they don't blow up in the wind. For lightweight materials, when weights are impossible, the designer Maureen Rose always installed a full dress lining because that way, if the dress went up, at least the lining would not. Thinking ahead is a key factor in retaining dignity. St Edward's Crown, which the Queen wore for her Coronation, weighs 54lbs. She walked around the Palace wearing it for days in order to get used to the weight.

Pencil skirts are out because they make getting in and out of cars, and walking up and down steps, difficult. Hat brims should not conceal the face and hats should be tethered with hatpins (covered in the same fabric) so you don't have to hold them on. Corseted and skirted bathing costumes are far more dignified than the 'camel's foot' version. Furthermore, most women wear the wrong bras, leading to conditions such as banana bosom or double bosom. The Queen is served by the Royal Corsetiere, Rigby & Peller, whose properly trained assistants know how to measure a bosom and devise a proper holding station for it whereby no unseemly movement will take place. Where footwear is concerned, the short-term benefit of looking taller than you actually are is soon negated when the shoes have to come off so you can take part in the events on offer, so stick to something you can walk in in the first place. The Queen can walk down multiple flights of stairs without looking downwards, a technique that requires some practice.

'Bag-woman' is not a good look. If you must carry a lot of stuff with you, avoid at all costs scrabbling in your bag for your mobile while it is ringing. It is a little known fact that all mobiles are set to ring only three times. This default setting is predicated on the assumption that all women will be frantically searching for the phone in their bag and will only get to it when it has stopped ringing. They then have to pay to ring back the caller. It is a lengthy procedure to have your mobile re-calibrated to ring ten or so times, but it will pay dividends in the long run. Incidentally, so that the Queen does not have to fish for her handbag at the end of a state banquet, it is fitted with a special clip so that it can be secured to a table.

The Queen has another big advantage over the rest of us. During a royal visit to Canada, the headline 'Why cool Queen still melts our hearts' appeared in *The Canadian*. The story ran, 'The temperature was in the mid thirties. Everyone but the royal couple was drenched in sweat. The Queen, who was carrying a heavy handbag and wearing long white gloves, never even produced so much as a hanky to dab herself. How is it possible?' I can answer that. It's because the Queen's body runs like clockwork and just as nature intended.

Dogs

Dogs are a nuisance and they have to be monitored at all times, but they more than reward your loyalty. If the Queen did not have dogs, how would she know that she was lovable for herself alone and not for her status? They're also good for your health. Patting them triggers the release of endorphins and other agents to keep you calm. In fact they can even help you get married. Both Ben Fogle and Davina McCall reportedly met their future partners when exercising their dogs in the park. Moreover, ownership of pets will help you out in tricky social situations. Having a dog gives you something to talk about to even the most dumbstruck of colleagues and acquaintances, helping you find common ground.

In some ways, dogs have the same appeal as doll's houses. Even if your own world is appalling, at least you can make one mini-world perfect. Ditto with dogs. You may not be able to make another human happy but you can easily make a dog ecstatic. And the well-trained dog is a living testament to the link between your effort and your reward – total obedience.

The Queen's gun dogs at Sandringham are so devoted to their mistress that it is reported that their ears start pricking when she is approaching, from as far as 20 miles away. In fact she regards dogs so highly that, in 1960, she gave her future brother-in-law, Anthony Armstrong-Jones, a wedding present of Doon, a black Labrador gun dog from the Sandringham strain founded in 1911. Back then, such a dog was worth £1,600, if you could get hold of one. (Sadly, Tony didn't like dogs.)

Eating

Only modest forkfuls make their way into the Queen's mouth; she chews the foodstuff to a paste and swallows the mixture. *Then* she speaks. Note, the Queen prefers non-fizzy drinks. Indeed it was Joan Collins who pointed out in her book *My Friends' Secrets* – about beauty, health and happiness – that the one secret shared by most of the elderly but still functioning beauties whom she interviewed was that they never had fizzy drinks. Fizzy drinks harm digestion.

Embarrassments

First, lavatories. They have traditionally provided the primary focus for social embarrassment. Double ensuite is the new status symbol amongst kleptocrat billionaires, but at Sandringham they famously have very few single bedrooms with ensuite baths. The royals have been known to use a notice saying 'Lavatory Under Repair' when they want people to bypass loos for various reasons.

Second, power cuts. When the Queen visited Jamaica in 2007 she stayed at Government House in Kingston. A power cut did not deter her from making stately progress down the staircase to the banqueting rooms, where she enjoyed a dinner entirely powered by candlelight and the headlights from cars driven up to the house. She made the most of the power cut, knowing from personal experience that they are a great way of reducing tension. In fact, power cuts are a popular way of making a party go with a swing. Suddenly nobody is embarrassed and everyone becomes childishly excited. People can get to know each other more freely and it gives something to talk about when the power is restored.

SUID-AFRIKA
KRONING 1953 CORONATION
2d
POSSEËL
POSTAGE
SOUTH AFRICA

Faith

When George VI underwent his Coronation, the Archbishop of Canterbury would not allow the event to be photographed or broadcast, in case men should listen to the ceremony wearing hats in public houses. Neither will I be trivializing faith in this self-help book. You can draw your own conclusions as to whether the Queen would have been able to do what she has done without being sustained by her faith. Suffice to say that the Duke of Edinburgh, who evidently has reservations about some of what the Church of England gets up to, has given us a clue in the conclusion of his own book, *A Question of Balance*. He wrote, 'religious conviction is the strongest and probably the only factor in sustaining the dignity and integrity of the individual'.

As we all know, the Queen allowed her Coronation of 1953 to be televised. The anointing of the Sovereign has the deepest significance during a Coronation. The recipe for the oil is secret but it includes orange flowers, roses, jasmine, cinnamon, musk, civet and ambergris. Under the authority of the Surgeon-Apothecary, the oil for the 1953 Coronation was made up at Savory and Moore Ltd by J.D. Jamieson, to a formula devised by Peter Squire. The consecration of the oil is arranged by the Dean of Westminster and performed by a bishop. In 1953 the Bishop of Gloucester, a former Canon of Westminster, performed the blessing. The cameras were denied a close up of the Queen's face, but those near the throne privately marvelled to witness a visible moment of spiritual transformation when the oil was applied. According to the Countess of Gainsborough, 'That oil really worked.'

It is also worth mentioning that Prince Philip, besides having an intense interest in spiritual matters, was the son of a deeply religious woman. His mother, Princess Andrew, founded the Christian Sisterhood of Martha and Mary in 1948 and lived as a nun wearing the habit of the Russian Orthodox Church, spending the last two years of her life in Buckingham Palace, where she died aged 84 in 1969. She was popular with staff, though considered eccentric. A chain-smoker, she could be heard coming through the Palace corridors by her coughing and was often in hospital with bronchitis.

Forgiving

A central tenet of Christianity is forgiveness and, if the Queen can forgive even Fergie, then we must all take our lead from her. Grudge-harbouring is unproductive and leaves no room in the heart for the new.

Lord Snowdon, for example, never forgave Colin Tennant for a social slight. On 21 April, 1956, the then Anthony Armstrong-Jones was employed as a photographer for the wedding of Lady Anne Coke (the 23-year-old daughter of the Earl of Leicester) at Holkham Hall in Norfolk: the groom, Colin Tennant, made him use the servants' entrance. Despite the fact that he had been to Eton and knew many of the guests present, he was not invited to luncheon.

It was the start of a lifelong, bitter enmity, and being on his high horse meant Tony could never go to the house Princess Margaret eventually built on Mustique, on land that Colin Tennant had given her. So Tony was robbed of the annual pleasure his wife enjoyed of lolling back in complete privacy, the baking sun beaming down, while being caressed by trade winds.

Frugality

As a child the Queen kept detailed accounts of her one shilling a week pocket money. As an adult the sequins and beads from her evening dresses are recycled on to new outfits. And heating bills for Buckingham Palace have been dramatically reduced by the ecosystem there, which has been in place for decades. A combined heat and power system, along with LED lights and double-glazed skylights, keeps costs down.

Kitty Kelley, the American biographer, purports to believe that Prince Philip was impressed by Merle Oberon's marble floors, silk sheets, cashmere blankets and gold-leafed beds; quite a contrast to the freezing palaces and scratchy tweeds he was used to at home. Don't be naive

Kitty, Prince Philip was just being polite. A sound knowledge of history and of the contents of the Bible would help promote in all of us a passion for sensible spending.

Nor is following fashion clever. Many landed families have found themselves ruined by their desire to follow fashion, building on huge extensions and constantly redecorating. The Queen has always hated fashion. 'Oh poor Britannia, she would have hated being Cool!' she remarked when Tony Blair was peddling the idea. In fact the Queen rejects new fashions, opting instead for the opposite stance, make do and mend. She even demolished 91 rooms at Sandringham but stopped when the cost of demolishment became too high.

Saving, unlike spending, can give one a satisfying sense of achievement. No matter what else happens, at least you can take pleasure from the thought of the metaphorical coins tinkling into your imaginary cash register – money which, through lack of careful husbandry and thinking ahead, would otherwise have gone down the drain.

Giving Your Own Parties

Even if you only give a drinks party just once a year, that will be enough to reassure your friends that you still care. Have it in summer in your garden. If you don't have a garden, have it in a local park. Prosecco from the nearby supermarket will be absolutely fine; people are always grateful to the person with enough dynamism and email addresses to set up the occasion.

Write clearly on the invitation '6–8pm'. People adore boundaries. They love being told when to go home, and they can use the party as a recruiting ground to then find someone to go and have something to eat with afterwards. There will be no bitterness that you have not provided food. This is all about having the administrative skills to lay on a ready-made scene.

If you were the Queen you could display more largesse. She hosts dine-and-sleep events at Windsor Castle and invites six married couples and eight singletons, and the Master of the Royal Household insists that tipping is not expected or desired. This leads guests to breathe a huge sigh of relief. The no-tipping policy is one of the chief factors in the success of hotel chains such as Sandals and Club Med and on ship cruises. What makes people more miserable than anything else, surveys have shown, is not knowing how much to tip.

Happiness

If you want to be happy for a day, go fishing; if you want to be happy for a week, go on holiday; and, if you want to be happy for life, serve others. On her accession in 1952 the Queen said, 'I declare before you all that my whole life, whether it be long or short, shall be devoted to your service.' Judging by her behaviour in the 60 years since she made this commitment, she meant what she said.

Try serving others, if you haven't already done so. The traditional remedies are always the best and this one is guaranteed to make you happy. By contrast, a life dedicated to serving oneself leads to the outcomes that befell Elvis Presley, Idi Amin, the Hollywood producer

Don Simpson and even the Duke of Windsor. And avoid being a Marie Antoinette, showing yourself to be superior to others. A dislike of being patronized may be one of the reasons why the Japanese refused help during the recent earthquake and why many Ugandans were so annoyed by the film *Kony 2012*.

In her own do-gooding work, the Queen, who always exhibits museum-quality authenticity on her walkabouts, does not tend to hug strangers or hand them money. Her style is to encourage and praise, and point to areas of practical help.

Health

Use it or lose it. The Queen has reliable horses and she communicates well with them to the extent that she brought her Burmese swiftly under control in June 1981 when a 17-year-old fired blank cartridges at her as she turned down Horse Guards Parade.

By continuing to ride, four days a week, she keeps up the capacity to do so. The requisite limbs remain used to the flexing. And by continuing to walk approximately four miles a day, she retains good use of her legs. In short, fresh air is a prerequisite and all the royals are known to go out in the kind of weather that most people would not dream of venturing into.

History

These days, it seems, our children have to teach themselves history as many schools have ceased to value the perspective it gives – as the life-enhancing tool it has always been, enabling us to keep calm and carry on.

This was not always so. When it became clear that Princess Elizabeth would one day inherit the throne, she was taught constitutional history by Henry (later Sir Henry) Marten, the vice-provost of Eton. These lessons began when she was 13. But you do not have to be royal to find Britain's history fascinating, and to feel proud that you yourself must hail from resilient stock if your family has weathered the storms of events such as the War of the

Roses, the Reformation, the Civil War, the Jacobite Rebellion, the craze for gambling and the agricultural depression that takes us up to the present day.

'History is shorter than we think,' observed the late historian Hugh Massingberd. 'Only some fifty generations separate the birth of Christ from today. Yet such is the mobility of the human race that the descendants of those of senatorial rank in the Roman Empire are now peasants and those whose ancestors were barbarians are now dukes and earls.'

Think back through what you know of your own antecedents. Is your potential quality of life better than theirs? People whinge about the difficulties of affording heating bills or foreign holidays, forgetting that their ancestors had no heating at all and their idea of a foreign holiday was a little rape and pillage in France. Yes, of course your quality of life is better! (What were the defining good characteristics of your antecedents? Have you inherited the same ones? Will you be passing them on? What mistakes did your ancestors make? Will you be making the same ones?)

Knowing Who People Are

No doubt a smartphone app is about to come on to the market that will tell us not only who someone is, when we point our device at them, but also when we last met them, and it will sound a warning note if we embark on a story we have already told them. But until such time we must accept that people get upset if we do not recognize them – admit it, you do too. Arch-flatterers say things like, 'I thought it couldn't be you; it must be your daughter!' but such tactics won't always wash. Therefore you must plan ahead.

If you are giving a party, find an excuse to give everyone name stickers as they come in. You can explain it by saying something like, 'We've got some ancient people coming and they far prefer it.' No one will grill you too intently or complain that it is too corporate; everyone will be secretly thrilled. And if you start work in a new office, sketch a map of the room and write on it the names of the people sitting at the various desks. Then, when you need to talk to them, just glance at your sketch.

Manners

The Queen is the standard bearer for classic British good manners. This is at the core of her popularity. The Queen has always enjoyed customs, rituals and ceremonies, but unlike the Chinese aristocracy, for instance, she has never allowed herself to be bedevilled by them.

Etiquette plays no part in the civility of which the Queen is the embodiment. Civility is a courtly art, practised by responsible well-wishers to ensure that others feel valued and respected. It has its roots in chivalry, one of the three rocks on which European civilization is built, the other two being Christianity and classical antiquity. Classical antiquity taught men how to think, chivalry how to behave.

The original medieval knights did not aspire to be anything other than more efficient killing machines than foot soldiers. But as the knight evolved into the 'gentleman', he also took on board the concept of the Renaissance man, Castiglione's courtier: the 'complete man' who was also required to be of fine appearance and perfect manners, at once a soldier, poet and scholar who knew about pictures and architecture, who could even ride to hounds.

The Indian Civil Service, a highly efficient administrative body, required candidates to have studied the classics at university and to have a certificate from the riding master at Woolwich. Candidates were expected to be courageous, to be faithful to the Church and to give service to the poor and weak, as well as being courteous to the fair sex and refraining from criminal activity. Thus the code of a gentleman, at its most basic, can serve as a substitute for Christian or humanist ethics. Which brings us to Dr Thomas Arnold of Rugby, the most influential Victorian headmaster of his day. He required of his boys, first, that they had religious and moral principles, second that they behaved like gentlemen, and third that they had intellectual ability.

Service, piety and modesty are the very basis of civilized behaviour and, without these core values, the Queen would be little more than a woman who happened to be richer or more powerful than other women. As you try to gain some of the happiness that the Queen herself must experience through the great joy her civility gives to others, bear these core values in mind.

Table Manners

Some of the tensest moments of life are linked to the festive celebratory occasions that should be the most enjoyable. The reason? Other people's table manners.

Those brought up to slurp, speak with their mouths full or chop meat into dog-food-like chunks before forking in the gobbets will cause no tension in houses where the same practices are observed. Should they marry into a household where the custom is to do the opposite, their partner will, in the fullness of time, feel suicidal. It is one of the reasons why society has traditionally frowned on marriages between people of contrasting rank.

But, as Britain is now characterized by very fluid social snakes and ladders, peace must be brokered in the table manner wars – and the most sensible solution is to copy the table manners of our own dear Queen, not because they display her high rank but because they have evolved out of practicality.

When the Queen entertains, footmen arrive at the left shoulder of each guest bearing each dish in turn and the guests help themselves. The footmen are alert and ready to shimmer forward if they perceive the merest flicker of desire for some ingredient not yet offered. In this way, each guest is delightfully satisfied. Not so all the members of the Royal Family. 'Life at Buckingham Palace isn't too bad, but too many formal dinners (Yuck!)' said Princess Di in a letter to a friend shortly after her engagement. The Queen has to preside over a number of state banquets each year. Invariably guests are offered a choice of chicken or vegetarian dishes so that no one needs to say 'No thank you.'

In a footman-free zone, it is up to us to pre-empt peevishness by making sure the plates of our neighbours to both left and right are fully loaded with everything they might want. It is in our own interest to do this as our neighbours will then be better company.

It is also in your own interest – if you are a man – to talk to the woman on your right for the first course and to the woman on your left for the second. It is almost like a team game and the one who lets the side down is the person who selfishly doesn't turn, causing the whole process to collapse like Dominoes. So turn you must, even if you have fallen passionately in love with the person next to you at the table.

Conversationally you will do better not to broach inflammatory subjects. It is bad for the digestion. You will find with the Queen that if you are about to broach a subject that is somehow unacceptable, she will quickly let you know, glaring in a certain way. Dinners are not debates, they are meant to promote a sense of inclusivity and harmony, and gratitude to the powers that be. Keep off touchy subjects and if you do feel like an argument, take out any aggression on your marital partner when you get home. Just be grateful that you don't have to entertain the likes of Idi Amin, Robert Mugabe and Nicolae Ceausescu, as does the Queen. How does she carry it off? By treating everyone in exactly the same way. Each state visit to Britain lasts exactly four days, no matter whether it's the president of the USA or of a tiny island, and she endures it for the good of her people.

In our own homes, we too have to 'process' partially savage people from time to time, for the general common good. One way to bear the ordeal is to render the room a pleasant blur by not wearing glasses or contact lenses, should you normally require them. Seating plans are clearly important to keep the 'savages' away from the 'civilized', as are the giant napkins used at royal banquets, but one way of training a grown savage into more considerate eating habits is to seat them close to children. In this way, the authority figure can constantly turn to the children and give orders such as 'don't speak with your mouth full' or 'remember to pass the salt and pepper to your neighbours'. The newcomer can pick up the rules by proxy and without taking offence.

Mystique

These days there is a prevailing sense that confession is healthy and good. 'There's no shame, we're all the same', is the catchphrase of Channel Four's *Embarrassing Bodies*. Well, up to a point.

Helpful as this groundbreaking television programme has undoubtedly been, the fact remains that, in terms of being attractive to or revered by others, romantically there is more to be said for mystique than exposure.

When everyone around us is drunkenly confessing to their foibles, perversions and physical defects, we are fascinated. But what we really find fascinating are those people who have not confessed at all. Like the Queen, they have a mystique that we would like to penetrate. And if we never do penetrate it, how much greater is that fascination.

Less is not only the new more, it is the old more. It is the eternal more. 'We must not let in daylight upon magic,' urged the economist and critic Walter Bagehot, who did not think that royalty would benefit from its public knowing the human details. And one reason for our Queen's enduring popularity is that she retains that mystique. We know she is a human but we do not know — and most of us certainly do not want to know — the details, thank you. Take a tip from her and keep your private details private. Do not tweet or Facebook or sell to the press stories connected to the less lofty side of your being human. Soul-bearing can and should be done, but not as a facet of gossip or titillation or for the short-term gain of drunken bonding.

The Queen hails from the generation in which stiff upper lips were the norm. Such a stance is currently unfashionable, but how much good does it do to talk to a non-professional about your problems? Train yourself to respond pleasantly but brusquely when friends ask how you are. In this way you will avoid the risk of misery-milking. Just reply, 'Really well. And you?' in a tone that implies you are not in the market for what, in olden days, was called an 'organ recital'. It does people no good to wallow in negativity, and it does you no good to be party to their humiliation and feebleness.

The Queen and Prince Philip obviously do have feelings but they keep them under wraps, and they are guarded, even with those with whom they are intimate. Mike Parker, a close friend of Prince Philip for 60 years, told Gyles Brandreth that 'Philip did not discuss his feelings, at least not with me. I did not know about him and Princess E until virtually the day of the engagement.'

Key Phrases to Put Off Nosy Friends

Two worthy rebuttals are:

'Let's wait till we see how things are next week.'

'I would love to gossip about it but there is

about to be a development and I'm sworn to secrecy, so let's talk again next week.'

Not Swearing

The television producer Sir Peter Bazalgette, who was responsible for the *Big Brother* series on Channel Four, claimed to believe that the F word had been 'rehabilitated by the young' and that broadcasting it should no longer be a problem. However, anyone who has looked into the art of neuro-lingual reprogramming will know that words and concepts with negative connotations are best avoided, as their incremental use may lead to depression and a sense of demoralization. If you are a swearer, you may find your own quality of life improves dramatically once you make the effort to forego the habit of littering your consciousness with 'negative confetti'.

Power Naps

The Queen could not achieve as much as she does without power naps. I cannot prove she has them but I know that Betty Parsons declared them integral to productivity. She said, 'You are never wasting time when you are recharging your batteries. You are gaining it ...'

Prayer

You may well not be religious but the Queen goes to church more often than anyone else in the country, save for professional clerics. When there, she prays – on her knees and with her eyes closed tight. It is none of our business what she prays about but we imagine, given her clear sense of duty, that she is praying for us. The point about praying is that it helps you to focus your mind on what you really want, and as you verbalize – either internally or aloud – even an atheist can see which requests are darned unreasonable, at which point make a fresh application for those things that you really need.

Processing People

Each of us now knows too many people – too many to 'process' or see. The Queen also knows too many but she's in the fortunate position of being able to give large parties so that no one may feel she has forgotten about them or doesn't care.

To speed things along during formal functions she never sits down and, for the same reason, stands throughout her monthly privy council meetings. The no-sit policy also means she avoids being cornered by bores. To avoid hurting the feelings of those she has met before, if she has perhaps forgotten their details, her Lord Chamberlain and his Comptroller ask guests if they have previously met the Queen, so that they can present them.

At her garden parties and investitures the Queen processes an average of one person per ninety seconds and yet no one feels short-changed. When meeting lots of people she clearly has a way of meting out her energy. As she admitted to Jackie Kennedy, who praised her stamina, 'After a while one gets crafty and learns how to save oneself.'

As ordinary members of the public, we do not have Comptrollers to effect this function for us. For instance, Nicholas Coleridge, the chairman of Condé Nast, calculated through his diary entries that by the age of 42 he had already met about 25,000 people. One way to find out who people are, when we see familiar faces looming but can't remember anything about them, is to keep a permanent petition in a pocket for some anodyne cause such as 'Save the Barnowls'. In this way you can greet each person who approaches by waving the petition saying, 'Before we even say hello, can I ask you to sign this?'

We are not all as popular as the Queen but some of us may still need to acknowledge an unfeasible number of people. Imagine, for example, hosting a drinks party with 150 people with a duration of just 120 minutes, thereby allowing but 40 seconds per person. If the correct tactic is not employed you will make more enemies than friends.

The correct tactic is to stand at the entry point. In this way, as each person comes in, they will be able to exchange words with you but will then have to push on into the throng, partly because of their natural need for refreshments and partly because of the pressure of those coming in behind them. The key point is that no one will ever feel slighted, because they will feel it was their decision to move on.

Punctuality is the
Politeness of Princes

'I was brought up to respect a soufflé,' said
Princess Margaret. But some people haven't
been. In houses where there are no footmen to
discreetly take your glass and stand meaningfully
at the door to indicate that you and your guests
must 'go through' and sit down, you sometimes
have to take firm action. Rather than screaming
like a fishwife at your guests, simply turn off
the lights in the room you no longer wish them
to be in. They will soon swarm through to the
dining table like moths to a flame.

And if you are one of the guests rather than the
host, remember, it is important not to distress
those people who have made an effort on your

behalf, especially if they have cooked something which will be spoiled if you do not turn up on time. Members of the Queen's generation are never late. The whole point of being on time, instead of starting to make phone calls to announce that you are running late at the moment when you are meant to have arrived, is that you thereby sidestep the terrible anxiety and guilt we have all got used to feeling since mobiles came in. Mobiles give the illusion that we have extra time. In fact they rob us of it. Take a tip from the Queen and let people set their clock by you.

Rising Above Things

We all have setbacks and the Queen has had more than one *annus horribilis*. It is easier not to take things personally when your *raison d'être* is to fulfil your duty, namely to improve matters for the greatest number of people.

Former *Vanity Fair* editor Tina Brown noted that the magic of the Queen's public appearances is that they are not personal appearances. They are, she said, 'acts of state, symbolic assertions of national identity, *ex officio* rituals, having nothing to do with individual characteristics and everything to do with impersonal roles assigned by tradition and that essence could not be affected by compliments or criticisms.'

Prince Philip put it another way while in

Ottawa in 1969: 'The monarchy exists not for its own benefit but for that of the country,' adding, 'We can think of better ways of amusing ourselves.' Sometimes he has got cross at the lack of understanding from certain quarters. 'You have the mosquitoes,' he told the people of Dominica once, 'we have the press.'

We must forgive the press for they know not what they do, but it was the media that egged on the decommissioning of the royal yacht *Britannia*, even though one drinks party on it in the presence of the Queen, while in Hong Kong, could result in a £3 billion contract for British workers.

The royals would prefer not to be victims of press harassment and spinning, and they think it demoralizing for their subjects to be given depressing and negative (and untrue) stories about them, but to give such stories the oxygen of publicity by suing would be an own goal. Amongst the allegations they have risen above has been the claim that Prince Philip had been rude to a deaf group and that he was therefore anti-deaf people. What many might not know is that his own mother had been deaf since he was a child. He was even Patron of the Royal National Institute for the Deaf. And for many years he has been the victim of serial stories suggesting a long affair with the actress Pat Kirkwood. In fact he met her just three times, twice in line-up parades after shows.

The Queen and Prince Philip see reticence as a virtue and self-control as a quality to be admired. They agree with Iris Murdoch that 'Happiness is a matter of one's most ordinary everyday mode of consciousness being busy and lively and unconcerned with self.' Furthermore, they are aware that sometimes people want to believe certain things about figures in the public eye and so the royals rise above it, perhaps most satisfyingly by not reading such stories. Prince Charles, for instance, invites his guests at Sandringham to name which newspaper they would like brought into their bedroom with their morning tea. He just requests that they do not bring the papers downstairs.

And if you have a good story, don't make the mistake of telling, let alone selling, it. That is undignified and people will believe what they want to believe anyway. (Prince Charles's parents thought he should not have given his story to Jonathan Dimbleby.) If you are forced to make a statement, simply say, 'Let us wait until we see what is the outcome of my enquiries.'

Christopher Silvester, a contributor to *Private Eye*, has this tip for British people who are involved in scandals – real or imaginary – which are picked up by the press. 'Go to America until it all blows over. No one in America has any idea who anyone British is. If there are no photographs to fuel it then it will all blow over very quickly. The only reason that the Antonia de Sancha and David Mellor scandal took off was because there were all those marvellous photographs of her to fuel the interest.'

The Queen refuses to give interviews, go on Oprah or discuss 'emotional' matters. She keeps calm and carries on. You too would do well to follow her example. Rise above things. Discuss them with one person, not every friend, because friends tend to ratchet up the misery ('Oh poor you!'). Become, like the Queen, a believer in post-traumatic growth rather than post-traumatic stress.

When friends are really pressing you to tell them about, say, your likely forthcoming divorce or potential redundancy, take a tip from the Queen and do not indulge in negative speculation. It is a little observed truism that friends are usually the wrong people to talk things through with. But in order not to offend when pressed, simply use the techniques outlined earlier and say, 'Actually there is something which is about to happen but I really mustn't talk about it yet because I have been sworn to secrecy. Give it a week or so and I may be able to tell you something *really* interesting.'

Romance

'Life without love is like a tree without blossoms or fruit.'

Kahlil Gibran

Romantic love has never been more difficult to find. The young have been groomed by vested interests and desensitized censors to delete romance from their emotional imaginations and the vacuum has been filled with torrid, barnyard-style coupling. These are the only images broadcast to them.

When did you last watch a film wherein romance was a key ingredient? There is plenty of sex, yes, invariably shown as happening moments after a couple meet and usually in a manner where the display of gross carnal appetites is presented as something to be applauded. But there is rarely a suggestion that sex is linked to love – instead it's all about irony, violence or perversion. There is no question of a slow, gentle courtship or suggestion that each participant is giving the greatest gift they can give ... no, full intercourse must take place immediately, ideally in an alley or while pinioned in a cupboard.

Against this landscape, how are the young supposed to search for and meet the right partner with whom they might aspire to a cosy, wholesome family life? Ultimately, it's what we all want. But finding a partner is tricky against such a background of 'perma-porn'.

Fifty years ago a society matron would have just steered young people towards someone they were likely to get on with. These days, while it might be going too far to say there is no such thing as society, there is not the same 'tribal' way of meeting someone, and yet marriage is all about safety and shared references. People do still like to marry the girl next door or the boy at the next factory bench; someone they have got to know slowly.

The Queen and Prince Philip got to know each other in the most natural way. They were cousins (more precisely they are second cousins once removed, and also third cousins through Queen Victoria and fourth through George III) and he would come to stay. She was vaguely aware of him as someone who would be at a house party and who was fun, and she could get to know him before there was any question of him pinioning her in a cupboard. They met when she was 13. Said Prince Philip, 'I was always around.' 'I once or twice spent Christmas at Windsor, because I'd nowhere particular to go,' he admitted many years later. 'I suppose if I'd just been a casual acquaintance it would have been frightfully significant but if you're related – I mean I knew half the people there, they were all relations – it isn't so.'

As Lord Mountbatten wrote to Prince Charles when urging him to marry a girl who would not start to become too selective by trying out too many different men, 'look at mummy. She never thought of anyone else after she had met daddy at the age of thirteen.'

Well we all know that Charles and Diana did not work out and, indeed, we know rather too many details about them, but the Queen and Prince Philip's marriage has worked. The starting points were good. They were not sullied by having passed through the hands of too many other partners, so there was still room in their hearts for romance, that almost forgotten key aspect of life – like music and food – which movie moguls want to rob our children of.

Meeting someone within your own home is the best place. Nightclubs are not. When you meet someone in the natural course of events, love has the chance to grow slowly. As Philip explains, 'I guess it really started in earnest at Balmoral in 1946,' recalling the pretty 20-year-old princess who still laughed at his jokes. She had not seen him since Christmas 1943 when he had chased her through the corridors of Windsor Castle wearing a huge pair of clattering false teeth.

Later, Elizabeth visited him at the Kensington Palace apartment of his aunt, the Marchioness of Milford Haven, and at the Chester Street home of the Mountbattens. He also took her to visit his cousins, the Brabournes, at their modest cottage in Kent and to Coppins, the home of the Duchess of Kent, in Bucks.

We don't all have giant houses to help us stage these slow events wherein we, or our children, can find partners. But we can, for example, hire a huge house from the Landmark Trust or the Helpful Holiday agency and bundle in as many people as possible. If everyone chips in, the holiday can be surprisingly much cheaper than a smart hotel.

Getting to know someone through serial and sober exposure, and allowing the build-up of passion to occur naturally, is far superior to going to a basement nightclub, dancing with a stranger and drunkenly giving him the greatest gift you can, and then finding that he does not call the next day. And why would he if you were only too happy to be used as a human spittoon? This is not liberation but self-harm.

By contrast, the house party scenario is the most fertile breeding ground for romance. There can be few more successful hunting grounds than the Scottish house party. With daytime spent in the wilds, buoyed by fresh air, and evenings beside the open hearth, love blossoms. Romantic progress can be made almost unobserved as the bachelor comes to associate the female with relaxation and enjoyment. There is none of the pressure for instant results that you will find in a nightclub. Try to arrange that your children meet likely future partners in a domestic setting and at an age when no sex can take place.

Dancing and Games

Dancing, especially reels and waltzes and others involving technique, puts a smile on everyone's face. Dancing in the old-fashioned manner – pinioned against someone else's body, only vertically rather than horizontally – was one of the original ways in which you could tell whether you fancied someone and whether or not the body chemistry was right. There was a sound traditional and biological reason for this type of dancing. If you want to help your children find a mate, or indeed to find one yourself, then a formal dancing party is the way to do it. Simply use recorded music and have a teacher in to rehearse the traditional steps.

At a house party you can play games in a way that puts everyone at their ease. The Queen is a dab hand at Racing Demon, jigsaws, charades, and so on. Playing Sardines enables you to get to know others at close quarter. The royals even had a game called Stone, which the Duchess of Abercorn explained to Gyles Brandreth: 'All the lights are turned off and you are absolutely still. There is fear and there is fun.'

The natural exposure under the same domestic roof means that artificiality of behaviour cannot be sustained, and layers fall away revealing the true person beneath. There is no comparison to that random nightclub encounter. But what about the number of guests? The ratio should be one-third women to two-thirds men. This is important. Co-education public schools such as Marlborough College, where the Duchess of Cambridge was groomed to become attractive and queenly enough to be married to a king, usually have a deliberate policy of no more than one-third girls. Apparently a weird effect takes hold when the ratio is 50:50; the girls go very virago and the men turn into wimps.

The recipe is therefore for each girl to invite three men who fancy her but in whom she isn't romantically interested. With any luck one of her single friends will fancy one of these three while she in turn will fancy somebody else's invitee. And finally, note that the ideal house party pays no attention to ostentation. Displays of wealth, taste, status or thinness are not key factors in the success of such an occasion.

Routine

The Queen's routine is fairly invariable. At 8am a tray with tea will be delivered to her bedroom and her bath will be run for her to the correct temperature, tested by thermometer to be 72 degrees fahrenheit.

Her clothes are laid out for her and her hairdresser will be present.

At 9am the piper plays beneath her windows and she walks from the bedroom, through her sitting room to the dining room, holding her Roberts radio, listening to the news of the day. She has cereal, toast and Oxford marmalade. At 10am her private secretary will arrive to discuss correspondence and state papers. Then she studies her briefing material.

If having a routine works for the Queen, let it work for you. Like continuity, it provides a yardstick against which we can measure ourselves. It breeds a sense of security and reassurance, and frees the mind for more taxing topics.

Scrapbooks

The memory is kept in instant repair through scrapbooks and photographs. The Queen does not need to keep a diary; it is effectively kept for her. Keeping a diary is vital for us because the unexamined life is not worth living and examining it is the key to improving it.

The whole reason why WeightWatchers works is that once you are writing down, in the little booklet which they give you, exactly how much you are eating each day, you can't be in denial. You see an incremental improvement, weight going down, intake going down. In the same way, the Queen can reread the diary of her last state visit to Jaipur, for example, and wonder how next time she can do things better.

In *The Seven Habits of Highly Effective People* (over 25 million copies sold), Steven R. Covey says, 'Writing is another powerful way to sharpen the mental saw. Keeping a journal of our thoughts, experiences, insights and learnings promotes mental clarity, exactness, and context.' Covey also promotes the power of writing good letters – communicating on the deeper, rather than on the shallow or superficial, level. It helps us get an update on ourselves. As E.M. Forster once said, 'How do I know what I think, until I see what I write?'

Smoking

The Queen was never one to become enslaved to a habit with such potential to compromise dignity. If you have made the mistake of starting to smoke, use nicotine replacement lozenges to help you give up. The chewing of nicotine gum is never acceptable.

Socializing

As I have indicated, now that we all know too many people we must process them in payloads. You do not have to have a pile of money, either old or new, to indulge in what are normally seen as very grand pursuits.

One of the fallacies about the English Season is that it must be very expensive, but anyone can go to any of the events and it is simply a matter of being well organized. It is one of the best forms of entertainment that England has to offer and is really good value for money. To attend Royal Ascot, for example, a first-timer need only apply between January and the end of March. It will cost about £60 per day, which compares favourably to spending two hours in an expensive restaurant.

Now that Ascot has giant screens everywhere, in line with other mass entertainment venues, punters can stand on the lawn, which is in many ways merrier, and see all the action. People rich and poor choose to picnic in the car park and meet up with friends, which is just as popular – because so much less corporate – as picnicking in a tent.

Men, if they do not have the kit for Ascot, can of course hire it. But you can also buy at charity shops, and it is well worth making a trip to Rutland to attend the annual clothing sale for cancer care charity Macmillan, where such outfits can be had for bargain prices. Women can easily get away with wearing a plain sleeveless shift dress which, if you have got the figure for it, you can buy from a high street chain. You will need a hat. Clever women get to know local dressmakers who can copy the good clothes of old.

Besides sporting events, picnics are also a fun way of avoiding expense while entertaining large numbers of people. Children are the key ingredients – it means you can have the picnic by day and that alcohol need not play too much of a part of the menu. Old-fashioned 'children's food' such as cocktail sausages, egg sandwiches, rice-crispy cakes and so on are perfectly acceptable. Adults love the excuse to indulge and take a trip down memory lane, remembering that the Enid Blyton characters of their youth were always declaring how much more scrummy food tastes when you eat it outdoors.

Host the picnic in your own garden or, failing that, the local park. The multi-generational aspect of a picnic is one of the keys to its success, and the multi-generational aspect of royal life in general is one of the keys to royal longevity. The Queen and her family used to go on the annual August journey to Balmoral on the royal yacht. They would cruise around the coast of the Western Isles of Scotland to Aberdeen, anchoring along the way in Caithness so they could picnic with the Queen Mother at the Castle of Mey.

Thinking Ahead

Entertaining may not deliver instant results, but it stores up credit for the future. Presenteeism matters. Like extended speed dating, there is no better way of getting the true cut of someone's jib than by actually spending time with them, no matter how many interviews you may have watched them give on television. State banquets are a case in point. When you have put yourself out for someone, made a fuss of them and welcomed them into the bosom of your home, it means that if and when the going gets rough over political or diplomatic issues – and the Foreign Office can be sure that invariably it will – you'll have brownie points in the bag. Your adversary will be better disposed towards you and more prepared to negotiate.

For this reason – quite apart from the fact that it makes your children very happy – it is always wise to attend school events such as Sports Day or fundraising quizzes. Needless to say, you should also go to your spouse's office parties, where you can meet those who will inadvertently affect your family's life. Make sure you're well informed. You're not going for the pleasure of the events themselves, but for the subtle and long-term benefits.

Tidiness ...

is one of the primary life skills. Like not reading the Sunday papers – which effectively gives you an extra day per week – it frees up so much time when you are able to put your hands on things easily. Crawfie, the Queen's nanny, revealed in her autobiography that as a little girl the Queen was compulsively tidy and was always arranging her shoes in tidy rows and also her collection of sea shells.

Timetables

The strict timetables necessary for the Queen's schedule also pay huge dividends in ordinary life. Why do you think children get so much more done at school than when 'working' under their own supervision? People enjoy having a structure imposed upon them, and in social life a lightly structured timetable will be secretly acceptable to most guests.

Being told that you have to wear black tie, for example, is paradoxically liberating because it removes all anxieties about under- or over-dressing at a stroke. Almost all Oxfam shops have racks of black tie suits waiting to be snapped up for about £15, many passed on by those who have 'gone on ahead'.

People love being told what they need to wear and what times the meals will be. Even if you told everyone to wear a velvet smoking jacket, that's no problem whatsoever. People will grumble but secretly they will be relieved, just as when you were a child and school uniform was the norm with absolutely no choice.

When anyone stays with the Queen, they are told exactly what to do when they meet her and what to bring. Rather than being threatened by the demands, or seeing it as evidence of control freakery, they find it a huge relief.

Treating Everyone the Same

Making others happy, as we have learned, is the key to making ourselves happy. Even if you only come across a few people per day: rule one is to treat each person the same way.

In 1979 there was a Commonwealth Heads of Government meeting in Lusaka, which Mrs Thatcher advised the Queen to boycott. The Queen refused to be politicized and went. As Lord Carrington recalled, 'It was a great eye-opener to see the way the Queen dealt with this. She saw each one of the heads of government individually, for exactly the same amount of time – and don't ask me how it was all worked out – and they all melted. From that moment on the whole atmosphere of the conference changed ... The secret was – and remains – that she treats everybody the same.'

Conclusion

'It is when you give of yourself that you truly give.'

Kahlil Gibran

The Queen described George VI at the unveiling of his memorial on the Mall in London in 1955 as: 'A man who by the simple qualities of loyalty, resolution and service won for himself such a place in the affection of all of us that when he died millions mourned for him as for a true and trusted friend.'

These words could equally apply to our own Queen.

And so, dear reader, I hope you will have enjoyed this study of our reigning monarch and that you will have absorbed from it some lessons which will help you, in your own quiet way, to become majestic too.

About the author

Mary Killen writes a weekly advice column for the *Spectator*. A journalist since 1984, her career began on Mark Boxer's *Tatler*. She has since written for the *Times*, the *Daily Telegraph*, the *Sunday Telegraph* and the *Daily Express*, as well as *Marie Claire* magazine and *Harpers & Queen*. She writes a monthly motoring column for *House & Garden* Magazine and a diary column for *The Lady*, and freelances for many other publications.